LIFE THE WAY I KNOW IT

"8 PROMISES TO LIVE BY"

BY TJ FREEMAN

Copyright ©2016 by Promising Purpose Publishing

"Life the Way I Know It" 8 Promises to Live By Author - TJ Freeman

Book Cover Design - Kreative Kage LLC
Book Cover Photographer- Stephen Midgett

Publishing Company ©2016 by Promising Purpose Publishing LLC (Cleveland, OH 44122)
First Printing, 2016
ISBN13-978-0692706879

Printed in the United States of America

TABLE OF CONTENTS

DEDICATION..5

CHAPTER 1 PROMISE TO DO THINGS THAT MAKE YOU HAPPY..8

CHAPTER 2 PROMISE TO L.O.V.E (LIVE OUT OF VICTORY EVERDAY)..23

CHAPTER 3 PROMISE TO FIND YOUR TRUE PURPOSE AND LIVE IN IT 32

CHAPTER 4 PROMISE TO NEVER GIVE UP......**44**

CHAPTER 5 PROMISE TO FORGIVE OFTEN AND TO NEVER LET YOUR PAST DICTATE YOUR FUTURE.....................................72

CHAPTER 6 PROMISE TO SURROUND YOURSELF AROUND POSITIVE PEOPLE **99**

CHAPTER 7 PROMISE TO OWN YOUR BEAUTY AND REMAIN TRUE TO YOURSELF..113

CHAPTER 8 PROMISE TO REMAIN THE AUTHOR OF YOUR LIFE STORY...128

ABOUT THE AUTHOR.................................134

<u>Dedication</u>

I would like to first and foremost thank God, for his favor and love he has shown over my life. My experiences have molded me into the woman I am today. I want to thank my children Taylor and Dallas for being my supportive team, by giving me continuous hugs and kisses on a daily basis and being my biggest motivators. I want to give a huge thanks to my mother Barbara for always being a listening ear, a supportive mom and one of my biggest fans throughout this journey. I would like to thank my sister Keisha and brother Desmond, for their endless support and love in all my endeavors, your support does not go unnoticed. Last but not least, I would like to thank all my family and friends for being there during the toughest times of my journey and providing me the mental an emotional support I needed along the way.

"One thing about life is that it does not come with instructions, giving us complete permission to make mistakes. Mistakes do not define who we are as people or what our futures hold. We decide upon those things. We have to be clear about what we want out of life, so that life can be clear on what to give us." – Tajuana Freeman

Life, the way I have experienced it and the way I have learned from it. When we think of our journey on earth, we oftentimes wish it didn't come with so many struggles or obstacles. However, I have come to see it differently, as some of my toughest struggles were my biggest life lessons. As I began to prepare an understand my true mission and purpose in life, I definitely needed to dig deep beneath the surface to find some answers. So I asked myself 'Why now?' The answer to that question is because life is meant to have lessons and lessons are meant to be learned. So on my journey to live better, learn more and love unconditionally, I had to first embrace the place where it all began, so that I could then start to focus on the path ahead of me. Thus far, I have learned that promises are meant to be made and then kept and are essential to govern your life by.

This book is an interpretation of life the way I know it to be. Here are eight promises I feel that we should make to ourselves in order to keep us structured and on the path to becoming the person who we desire to be! Join me on this journey of experiences and let us reflect along the ride.

◆ **Chapter One** ◆

"Promise to do things that make YOU happy."

"Don't wait around for other people to be happy for you, any happiness you get, you've got to make yourself"~~ Alice Walker

I wish I had made this promise to myself ten years ago. It would have eliminated a lot of unnecessary pain and confusion from my life. Happiness is the mental or emotional state that is defined by positive and pleasant feelings that can range from contentment to joy. Even though happiness is a feeling, it is

also a choice. A person has to choose to be happy. For many years, I involved myself in things that I thought would make me happy, such as relationships, jobs, materialistic items and actions. I remember feeling down and sad about my life, always saying things such as "I need a companion to make me happy" or "If I only had X amount of money, I would be happy," but boy, was I wrong! Not long after, I went on a search to find happiness because that is what I felt I needed to fulfill my life. Little did I know, I was actually confusing happiness with comfort, not knowing that happiness starts with me first. My first mistake was looking for happiness, happiness is something you have to have within yourself, and you cannot get that from another person or thing. They can undoubtedly do things to add to your happiness, but if you do not create and carry happiness within yourself, you will be disappointed every time. Unfortunately, I did not learn that until later in life.

So what is so important about being happy? Happiness can oftentimes can be that breath of fresh air you need in order to get through life and make better decisions. In my past, every relationship I was in, I remained a conformer, no matter the cost. I would suppress my own feelings in order to make my companion happy or to eliminate any drama. I would avoid voicing my opinion to keep the peace, even when it was clear that I should speak up. I was suppressing my feelings, just for the sake of being in a relationship.

Perhaps because of this tendency, I always found myself being controlled in relationships by people who I thought loved me. I always wanted to know why I was attracting such people. Could men read me and notice that I was vulnerable to the idea of having a husband and kids and would do whatever it took no matter the cost? What I soon began to learn was that these controlling relationships were actually costing me more than I ever imagined.

I can recall being in a relationship with a guy that always caused me more pain than pleasure. It was mostly internal. In the beginning he used his words to put me down and lower my self-esteem. It was almost as if he got satisfaction from hurting my feelings. He always said negative things to me, but in the same breath, he would say that he loved me and wanted to marry me. Strange, right?

Life has a way of bringing people into your life that clearly should not be there permanently. It is our job to know who is temporary and seasonal, but when you are not sure about your worth, figuring out who is for you or against you can be a hard task. This guy would always seem to be in competition with me. He watched my every move, not to admire my accomplishments, but to find errors in all that I did. It wasn't long before his negative nature turned into controlling me and verbally abusing me. I was sleeping with the enemy and praying with the devil. As time went on, I became conditioned to accept the negative things he was saying.

I told myself "I guess I will not amount to anything!"

I have always been a reserved person. I stayed to myself and didn't share the things I was going through. I told myself, "What goes on in the household, stays in the household and it's nobody's business." In spite of this, I often asked myself "How long will I have to endure this? Am I worth it? Is this what goes on when you are in a REAL relationship?" When we envision our future, it is important to have an idea of what that looks like. We can't afford to walk through life without a plan or a vision for ourselves. Having no vision leads us to entertaining ideas and doing things that serve no purpose, and will cause us more pain and heartache than good. You can never guess what life will throw at you, but when you have a vision, you have an eye for what looks right. This vision must be strong and reliable because it must endure the toughest of obstacles, as I learned.

For the most part, I enjoyed my life and lived in the moment. I trusted whoever told me they loved me, until one night when we went out to a friend's party. We always went places as a couple, and to this day I'm not sure if that was a controlling mechanisms or just our normal, but that is what we did. At this party, we had fun in the beginning along with our mutual friends. My boyfriend, at the time, was drinking heavily, as usual. He came up to me and told me that a guy across the room was staring at me. He asked me if I knew him, and I said, "No." He kept persisting that I must have known him. He kept saying, "I saw him talking to you and he keeps staring at you."

Despite my insistence that I did not know him, he became angry and insisted that we leave the party. When I disagreed, he pulled me out of the club. We began arguing on the way to the car and the whole ride home. Once we arrived at our apartment, he began pacing the house in a fit of rage because he thought I was cheating on him and that I was lying about knowing the guy at the party. I can remember getting scared. I had never seen him that mad before.

When I picked up my phone to text my friends to let them know I had made it safely, he took my phone and banged it against the wall until it broke in half. That is when I knew it was about to be more than an argument. He began yelling and screaming, pinning me against the wall, pointing his hand in my face. He started throwing me into the walls, convinced I was cheating on him. I tried to escape through the front door, but he threw me back and dragged me upstairs.

I remember walking into the bathroom when suddenly he came up behind me, put his hands around my neck, and began choking me. He banged my head on the window and continued choking me until I blacked out for a few seconds. I can remember looking into his eyes and seeing all red; a lifeless an evil look in his eyes. How could someone who claims to love me touch me in this manner? I could have suffocated to death, leaving my only child, at the time, behind. I thank God that the neighbors heard the fighting and called the police. He went to jail that night.

I have spoken with many women, many of whomlet this sort of behavior go on for 5-10 years with the same or multiple relationships. What can we do to gain the strength to overcome this situation? Unfortunately, there is no one solution to this issue, but I can tell you what I did to overcome it. I was faced with the option either to press charges or to give him another chance at hurting me again. The fact that we love and are nurturing creatures by nature does not make it any easier. We always want to see the person we love change for the better, but there also comes a point when you have to love yourself even more. I knew in my heart that if I stayed in the relationship, I would do myself more harm than good, so I decided to press charges an end the relationship.

I learned from my past that I had compromised many things, including my happiness. On the inside, I was unhappy in my relationships. Now I understand why controlling men were attracted to me. It dawned on me that my past is not what I imagined happiness to look like. I was purposely ignoring the signs and not playing by the guidelines it takes to live a fulfilling and purposeful life.

The first step is to do things that make you happy! That sounds easy enough, right? It may seem so, but it is not as easy as it seems. If it were, a lot more people would be happy in this world. It will take work to get this step done and done correctly. It is so easy to fall back into old habits, but you can do this!

Next, you will want to make choices about your life that will actually give you the happiness that you deserve. Choose to do activities because YOU want to do them! Choose a vacation, because it is where YOU want to go! Go to a restaurant, because YOU want to eat there! There are so many new and different things out there that you have probably never tried because you were so busy living for other people. NOW is the time to live for yourself and do anything and everything that will make YOU truly and purely happy!

As I said, it will be difficult and it will take time to make the adjustments necessary to do this. After a while, though, it will become a part of your normal life. You will begin to make choices based on what is best for YOU automatically. You will begin to do things because it is what you want and what is best for YOU! Imagine being happy all of the time! Do you think that you could actually enjoy being happy all of the time? How nice would that be? I bet you are thinking that it is not possible, but it is. Even through good or bad days, you can still be a happy person.

Now, do happy people have bad days?

Absolutely! Do happy people get upset about things occasionally? Of course! Life obstacles are inevitable; the difference is that a person that is happy will acknowledge hurdles in their life and not see them as an ending, but rather as a beginning, a beginning toward a brand new start, a beginning toward positivity.

The first thing I had to acknowledge was that men or things should not be allowed to complete my life or to fill any voids. I am responsible for that part, not a man. Once I began to learn my true worth and the power I held within myself, I could, at that moment, begin to make better conscious decisions about my happiness.

Never settle when it comes to being in a relationship. When it is your time, you will know it. A lot people are single, not because they are not worthy of a mate, but because it is not their time for a relationship. Do not use your time as a single person to worry about why you are single; use it has an opportunity to become a better you. Use this time to work towards achieving those goals you set, doing things that make you happy and working on whatever flaws you feel you should change about yourself. It is important that while you are in this self-changing process that you do not aim for perfection because, unfortunately, perfection does not exist. Aiming for perfection is what gets many people in depressed moods, because they are aiming for something that is impossible to achieve.

Sometimes we have a tendency to rely on other people to make us happy. However, that is a lot of pressure to put on other people, and, truthfully, they probably will not know what we need. We are the ones who know about those little things that will make a difference and improve our moods. We have the capability of making ourselves happy. There are five simple things you can do to make yourself happy:

1. Make a list of things for which you are thankful. If you think about everything that is

good in your life, then you will realize all of the things that can make you feel grateful. Soon, you will start to see the good things around you, rather than focusing on those things that might not be going the way you wish. Thankfulness can also change your perspective. You can turn negative things around by being thankful for the opportunity to solve problems and overcome difficulties. This in turn will make you even stronger.

2. Spend time outside. Go for a hike, walk around your neighborhood, or go play at the park. Spending time in the sun not only increases your vitamin D, but connecting with nature can make you feel calm, relaxed, and happier. Physical activity will increase your energy levels, and play will release the carefree kid in you.

3. Spend some time volunteering. There are many places that need your help. Volunteering your time to your favorite cause has many benefits. First, you see that you are needed an appreciated, which in turn builds your self-esteem. Second, volunteering makes you a little more grateful for the things in your life, both physical things and people.

4. Buy something for someone else. They say it is better to give than to receive. Seeing the smile on someone's face when you hand them a gift is actually contagious. Without thinking about it, you will start smiling as well!

5. Most importantly, smile! The more you smile, the more you feel like smiling. Your smile is contagious. You smile at others, and they smile back at you. Before you know it, you have the whole world smiling with you.

The point is, you have the capacity to make yourself happy, nobody else does. No matter what you do, focus on those little things that make a difference in your world. Be thankful for what you have, and appreciate yourself and others. The only way to be happy is to make a promise to yourself that you will do what it takes to maintain your own happiness. Then do it.

"LIFE THE WAY I KNOW IT" 8 PROMISES TO LIVE BY | FREEMAN

Chapter 2

Promise to L.O.V.E (Live Out of Victory Every day!)

Live each day as though you have already won!
Love doesn't hurt, so don't believe it when it does.

What does it mean to live out of victory every day? In my opinion, it means trying to do things from a good heart. Loving yourself first and loving those around you are the initial ingredients you need in order for the idea to work. Each new day is an opportunity to be a better you and be a positive

23

example toward others around you. Victory is important to be lived out through your decisions, your job, your family and friends. You would be surprised how better this world would be if people lived through love, instead of hate. Love unites our families and communities and helps bring value and self-worth to our youth. We have to use love as a mechanism to bring about healing in our lives and in others.

Living out of victory every day pertains to our relationships as well. For years, I could never understand why I always dreamed and desired to have a family, house and that classic family dog. My mission, when I entered relationships, was to get married and to be with my husband forever. Now, it is okay to have marriage as your ultimate goal, but it is not healthy to go into every relationship thinking that every person is going to be the one to marry. When you find the right person, it will feel right. It is important to learn as much as you can about people when you first meet them. If you learn that they are not the right one for you, do not waste time because time waits for no one.

As years went by, I started thinking to myself "I am missing a big component when I meet guys. I'm skipping the dating part!" So many of us are doing this. What is dating? The term is subjective. Dating can mean different things to different people. Dating occurs when you meet someone and decide to invest time in trying to get to know them. It is a time for you to go out with a person to learn more about them and to see if you and that person are compatible enough to be in a relationship. It is conversations and social activities. It is the step you take before beginning an official relationship and, in turn, a marriage.

What have I been doing all this time? For my first few relationships, we entered the relationship before we ever dated. We thought we knew each other and made the commitment without taking the dating step. Now, I wish I had not skipped this step so easily.

Looking back, I wondered, what was the rush? Everything that involves your heart should be done in processes. Something as important as family, sex, and love should go through some stages, instead of jumping right to the end goal. If we give all those things to a person we think we like, but we don't take the time to get to know them through dating, the end result can cause a lot more pain than pleasure.

Let me explain something I realized about dating; it helped me to make more conscious decisions throughout the courting process. Dating is a free process that we can take advantage of; to only add to a relationship if it is worth it. I do not hear people saying, "I should have never dated him before I married him, it was a waste of time!" It's what you do on the dates that make them valuable and worthwhile. Creating a clear connection and bond cannot be replaced. Use dating as a filter for the things that are good or not good for you, so that you do not make all those painful mistakes that have to do with love, your heart and time.

You never want to make a habit of wasting time, because you can never get that time back. Enjoying the dating process is probably the easiest and most carefree part of the relationship. Learn what he or she wants from you and from life, so there is no confusion later. Also, determine whether you are falling for that person or just lusting after them.

Here are some signs of both:

<u>Signs of Lust</u>

- Interested in sex more than conversations
- You only share minimal information about yourself
- Conversations are filled with desires instead of real life discussion

- Being interested in a person's physical appearance more than anything else
- No physical touching such as hugging or cuddling after sex (he/she just leaves)
- You overlook a lot of their faults, even if you know you can't deal with them long term

Signs of Love

- You want to spend quality time with the person
- You want to introduce them to your family and friends
- You want to connect and intertwine your lives with each as much as possible
- The person motivates you to be a better person

- You want to share all your personal interest and goals

I am guilty of confusing love and lust when I entered into relationships. Lust is a purely physical attraction and it does not have any lasting effects. It is when you are sexually attracted to someone an only want them to be next to you physically. It is a magnetic feeling, but it is not love. Be careful not to confuse the two. I always had a particular type when I began dating; he had to be a particular height, have a particular look, personality, and income level.

However, after having unsuccessful relationships with people whom I categorized as my type, I figured it was time to try a new method. How about still having standards, while giving people who are not your type an opportunity to show you about themselves and show their strong interest in you. Scary? Nervous?

Well love is all about taking chances, so it is worth a shot, wouldn't you think? Lust is not the glue that holds relationships together, long term-love and communication are. The two terms will have you entertaining different perspectives on life.

This is why it is so important to be clear on what you want out of life. My mom always told me "A man should love you more than you love him initially, because as woman we can catch up to their love." Take a moment to consider your own thoughts on that advice.

As humans, we tend to base many of our decisions about our relationships on the fear of being single. There is nothing wrong with being single. It is usually what you do with your time as a single person that gets you into those slumps. We were designed to procreate and to be with another person, so it is no wonder that so many people do not want to be single and yearn for a soul mate. Though that may be true, we shouldn't let that desire or need for companionship make us compromise our happiness and future goals, because we will regret it in the long run. Get to know yourself first and learn who you are as a person, so you can enter a relationship with no filters. Grow to be your own best friend and biggest supporter.

Know your worth and what makes you valuable, so that you create a life of standards that you can become accustomed to living by.

Also, aim for victory through your trials and tribulations. Although I feel being a parent is one of the most rewarding jobs in the world, being a single parent also has many challenges. You never know how strong you can be until you are put into certain situations. Being a mom of two children and working in corporate America is a challenge. What I learned is that it is important to have consistency and time management as core skills to balance it all out.

Since there is no such thing as a perfect mother, it is okay to make mistakes. There is no parenting manual with all the answers, some things can only be learned through lessons and experiences. Keep in mind that these lessons and experiences will be what shape you as a person, as well as your child- and that is one of the most valuable journeys you can take.

Chapter 3

Promise to Find your True Purpose and Live in It

"It's time for you to move, realizing that the thing you are seeking is also seeking you". Iyanla Vanzant

So how do we find our purpose in life? Why do you believe you were created? If your answer is, "I don't know" that is fine, but let's start today to find that answer. Our purpose on earth is as important to our lives as food and drink is important to nurture our body. Without our true purpose, we are merely walking through life without a clear objective. It is just like the saying, 'if you don't stand for something than you will fall for anything!'

For example, when you live without purpose, it may be easier for you get distracted. If you are unclear about your worth and value, obstacles are harder to overcome.

Have you found your purpose in life? Do you know what you were put on Earth to do? Are you here to just do some mundane job and live and breathe work? Or do you think that you were put here in order to help someone or do something extraordinary? I believe all of us, including you, were put here for a reason! You need to find what you are good at and live the life that you are supposed to be living. Are you good with children or creating things or helping others? Take a good look at what you are good at and then find a purpose for your life from there. Take a few classes at a local college or community center and see what you enjoy. Your possibilities are endless.

How do you determine what your purpose on earth is? Once you establish the meaning of your purpose, you can then look to ourselves and decide how you want to express that meaningful purpose in this world. So ask yourself a few questions: what do you love to do? What is something in this world that, even if you're sick, would get you out of bed? What helps you face your fears and does not always make you comfortable, even though it makes you happy?

One of the main steps to finding your purpose is being able to be genuine and not self-centered in your interpretation of God's word. If we do things that are not of God, then we will make decisions based on our own earthly beliefs, which will revolve around you, and guess what: It is not all about you all the time. Once you can exist in the world for someone other than yourself, you are that much closer to your purpose. Following our purpose is scary. It makes us nervous because of the fear of failure as well as the fear of not being accepted by others. It is true, however, that when you are following your purpose, all those fears of rejections and pain have to be thrown out of the window, because the ultimate goal is to follow God's word and praise and worship his name.

Another step in finding your purpose is to remove yourself from what the world has said you are supposed to be. The process of stepping outside of your box is important, in order to explore all of the options that are available to you and to not limit yourself on all that life has to offer. The box was put into place so you would never have to face fears or be uncomfortable, but the box also keeps you from your purpose. Sometimes, we tell ourselves that we should stay in certain life situations because they are comfortable.

Well I beg to differ. Sometimes we confuse comfort with happiness, so it is important to not rely on the normal box activities for comfort, because there is a purpose out there with your name on it. Also, we cannot expect our purpose to fall in our laps. We have to do our way to our purpose and not just think our way to it. You must put your mind to it and then do it.

We also have to reprogram our minds from thinking that we are supposed to do this one super almighty position, because the truth is that there are a lot of things we are good at, so find your passions and those will lead to your purpose. Action is the best way to help yourself work towards your purpose. For years, I struggled with finding what my true purpose on earth and I began to feel "stuck" and unworthy, because I did not know why I was here. I read that the two most important days in our life are the day we are born and the day we find out why.

That being said, if you are struggling with the 'why' portion, then you are more prone to feeling depressed or stressed because you feel like you are living a pointless life with endless roads of struggles. It is harder to wake up in the morning when you live a life with no drive. Days get harder because you are not sure why you are even in this world and what you should be doing with each of your days.

A lot of our youth in the community that are either making bad choices or committing acts of violence, are still struggling with the "why" portion of their life. They are struggling with defining their worth and are choosing the views of man instead of God. Instead of learning their purpose, some of our youth have accepted the negativity or life that they think they suppose to live, no matter how confusing and painful it might be.

When I was younger, I thought long and hard and could not find my purpose. It seemed that no matter what new task or career I focused on, it was not fulfilling to me. The majority of my life, I struggled going through things such as the corporate world and college, on a mission to try and "figure life out". Life was a constant struggle for me and I could not figure out why or what my road to greatness was supposed to be. I always felt I was supposed to be a lawyer, to help with our legal system and to help people with legal issues, but the more I became knowledgeable about that field, the more I felt that it was not what I was meant to be doing.

No matter what job I held, if I did not believe in its mission, it did not feel like my purpose. It is a strange feeling because you may feel like you are doing everything right, but until you align yourself with God's word, all your work will feel either insignificant or pointless.

When I was working with a county agency helping abused kids, I had that famous 'Ah ha!' moment. I realized what motivates and drives me. I realized that anything involving helping youth or adults overcoming obstacles and helping them build confidence was my passion. As a result, I started my own nonprofit organization to help at-risk youth overcome obstacles and I became a Certified Life and Confidence Coach in order to help people gain their footing in life and find the tools within themselves to go to their next desired personal level. It is important to understand the "why" behind the actions you choose to. The "why" portion will lead you to a clearer understanding to what motivates you!

Finding my purpose took a lot of sacrifice as well as walking away from what was comfortable, sometimes even what was paying me income, to learning to walk towards the unknown. This was especially true when the unknown was made up of what I loved to do. It felt like I was taking a huge risk and based on the pay cut I took, I started to believe it was, but nothing could compare to the feeling of knowing that I had a divine purpose on this earth. Today, instead of waking up each morning, dreading getting out of the bed, I can hardly wait until I leave for work every day. Now that I know my mission and purpose, life has so much more value.

When you walk with purpose, you walk with confidence even through the storms, because you know your purpose and that God is favoring your life. Get clear about your vision and mission and nothing will separate you from that.

"WHAT IS MY PURPOSE IN LIFE?" Is a question many people spend their entire lives trying to answer. No matter what your age is or what stage you are in, you too can find your purpose. You do not have to spend your entire life searching. If you search hard enough and in the right places, your life purpose will be waiting.

When thinking about your purpose in life, first analyze the situation you are currently in. What goals are you pursuing, and for what reason are you pursuing those goals? Are you pursuing any goals at all? Many people decide to go on certain paths because of their surrounding influences. The people around us constantly pressure us to do things that are more favorable to their own expectations. This influences the personal decisions most people make. Many people make decisions that will please others, and not themselves.

Another step in finding your purpose in life is to stop living to meet the expectations of others, and live for your own desires and goals. This may be difficult for many people to do, but doing this will help you to find your own personal path, even if you do not figure out that path immediately.

To find this purpose, you should examine your life, the things that you enjoy in your life, and the goals you have. By doing some self-reflection and soul searching, finding your purpose in life will be a goal that you can easily attain. Once you find your purpose in life, you will be able to live passionately and confidently in your path.

As I said before, the possibilities are endless for you and your life. If you haven't done something and it seems interesting to you, then try it out. You are the only one that is holding yourself back. Do not be afraid to tackle anything head on and you will be very successful. Even if it takes you a while to figure out what your purpose in life is, you will be finding out many new things about yourself as a person. Everything that you find out can be used as a tool, so you can create a life that is unique to you, and you alone.

God has a plan for your life and plans to prosper you in whatever He has called you to do. We must know that we are not an accident in the world and that God has a plan for us. It is even stated in the bible. Jeremiah 29:11, "For I know the plans I have for you, declares the Lord, plans to prosper you and not to harm you, plans to give you hope and a future."

Chapter 4

Promise to Never Give up! You have come too far! Knowledge is power!

"Whatever you fear most has no power-it is your fear that has the power. The thing itself cannot touch you. But if you allow your fear to seep in your mind and overtake your thoughts, it will rob you of your life". ~~ Oprah Winfrey

Ever since I was in 6th grade, I said I was going to be a lawyer and help others in my community, through life's obstacles and their legal issues. I always wanted to help people in some form and I love debating about current political topics, so I felt my career path could only lead me to being a lawyer. As I began on my journey in life towards my career, things seemed to begin taking a toll on me. I started to have health issues and I still was a part of draining situations revolving my relationships and friendships. I was under a lot of pressure and subsequently, it caused me more harm than good. I had to put my journey to becoming a lawyer on hold, and looking back, this decision was such a painful part of my life. There I was again, letting life and people come between me and my dreams an aspirations. I felt empty; like I once had answers, but now I was closed in a room with unanswered pressures that I had to deal with first.

I looked in the mirror and saw a beautiful black woman on the outside, but under that layer a woman who also felt empty on the inside. The emptiness had nothing to do with material things, because I had plenty of that. What I was void of, was the things that I could not see or touch that still made up a part of who I was as a person. It was something that I could not put a price on.

For those next coming months, I stayed to myself, not inviting or allowing anyone into my life.

One day, I was writing in my journal and I started off an entry by writing "What is my purpose on earth and why am I here?" I just knew it was more than what I was doing at that time. The search for myself soon began, but I still needed answers on where I should start this time, because just making the statement "I will start with myself" was too vague. Instead, I decided to start with my heart. The heart that helps shape and mold my decisions. Which way am I going? I'm moving fast, but I'm still not where I want to be in life. I took a long life pause and began reflecting.

As you will notice throughout this book and even through the life storms, I always faced my obstacles by reflecting. I found that, sometimes, you have to seclude yourself and look inside you if you want to start figuring things out. I immediately started with who I was allowing near my heart.

As I mentioned before, even though I was a reserved person, the idea of having a family often got me into relationships that were not for me. After

I made the decision to leave my daughter's father, I moved back to my home state. Even though it was a tough decision to make, it also was the most stress-free experience I'd had since I had become pregnant. I was now surrounded by people who loved me and who cared for my daughter and me. It was not a complete family to me, but unconditional love was there. Once I was away from the toxic relationship, I was able to start the healing process.

There is no such thing as healing from hurtful relationships that you are still involved in. In the beginning, my days were filled with darkness. I had many hurtful memories and many decisions I would have to make in the next few weeks, once my child was born. I began questioning myself and saying things like "Maybe I should have stayed to keep my family together, even if I did risk jeopardizing my happiness" or, "It's my fault I'm a single mother, because I left. Am I a bad mother already to my unborn child?" I was consumed with pain, stress, and unanswered questions. In my down moments, I tried to self-medicate, because I did not want to admit or tell my problems to anyone, because that was how I dealt with my issues.

Whenever you get involved in a situation where you just want out of this earth, you have to start talking to yourself in the mirror. I wish I would have read a motivational book or that somebody had told me all of this earlier on. I recommend you look in the mirror at yourself and say out loud, "Dear Self, look at my life; how did I get here?" Do not take too long pondering on that question, but you go to the source of the problem,so the healing begins.

Now that you have recognized that you are in this situation, what now? While I still had some questions about some of my life events, what I focused on was what I was confident about and what was positive in my life. Please do not say you have nothing positive to say, because the fact that you are breathing and were given an opportunity on earth is worthy of being on your positive list. I feel that whatever we condition ourselves to believe, we can control the results and goal of making life work for us instead of against us. We cannot control every aspect of life, but what we can control is how we react when life throws us lemons. We can either make lemonade or we can we soak in the sourness of life.

Life is all about perspective; what you believe you can achieve, and your opportunities are limitless. If you are reading this book, then you have come far.! Stay rejuvenated, motivated, and on a mission. There is so much more of life we have yet to see and achieve. If you were like me and experienced some form of pain, heartache, or disappointment when you were a child, remember that we can either live in that moment or learn to live past that moment, that keeps holding us hostage in our own life.

We have to know that we are not the things that happen to us. They are chapters in our life story, but since we have the pen, we have the power to change our lives for the better and write new chapters that reflect our new life story. Sounds simple, right? Absolutely not. But it's definitely attainable and worth the change. We cannot remain victims of our own life. We have to face life head-on and refuse to take no for an answer.

pity parties are not allowed. We are born conquerors, so it is important to not let anyone else write our story for us. We must remain the authors of our own stories until our time is over. When we reach that point, we will have made an impact on the world the way we wanted.

I cannot stress enough how important it is to have a clear mind, so if you are in a draining or stressful situation, it's important to remove yourself from that situation, so that you can continue on your journey of your true purpose. The key to recognizing road blocks is to pay attention to the people that are the closest to you. Those are the ones that can hurt or impact you the most. Even though some people are designed to come into our life to steer us off our path, it is our job to stay focused and to keep going and to never give up. At the end of the day, we cannot blame anybody for our failures but ourselves. We must remain holding the pen to our life book and keep all the power that is within us.

One of the first things you need to do is to promise yourself a few things. They are not difficult or very time consuming and they can even be fun once you get used to doing them. Some of them may seem difficult, but that is only because you have not done them before. They are going to help you to change your outlook on life and live life for yourself. They are going to help you become a positive and loving person, no matter what obstacle comes your way. The sooner you get started with these few steps, the happier you will be and the better your life will be.

No one should ever give up in life. I know life can be difficult at times, but that is just how it is. We have what it takes to conquer anything that comes our way. Whether it is job loss, losing a family member or a friend, losing our home or car, we can find a way to keep going. Yes, it will take some time and lots of energy and tears, but it will happen. You just need to tell yourself that it is okay to move on and keep going and that it is okay to be yourself. It is okay to grieve. It is okay to feel sorry for yourself for a little bit, but you find a way to change the situation. If the situation is a loss of a job or house or car,you find a new job, house or car. You have the ability to do all of that. You might not think that you do, but it is true. You may also find that the new job might even be better than your old one. The same goes for the house or car.

Any new opportunity that comes your way will always be better than what you have in your life at the moment. If you have wanted to move to a new area, maybe this is the time to take advantage of that dream. Maybe the bad thing happened so that you would do what you wanted for a change. Remember, there is always a reason why something happens.

If the bad thing that happened was a loss of a

family member or friend, then it will be more difficult to move forward. You will feel this loss to your core and it will take time for you to move on. This may take years and even though that sounds horrible, it is not. The reason it will take many years is because grieving is a process and it has many phases. Each phase is meant to give us a new meaning; a new meaning as to why it happened, a new meaning on how you can live without the person, or a new meaning of how you react with each passing day. Time needs meaning. Our lives need meaning. The person we are now is not going to be who we are a year from now, two years from now or even ten years from now.

We might find that the meaning that makes the most sense to us this year is not the one that will make sense to us next year. We are always growing, always changing. We need to look at who we have become and make sure that who we have become is the best person that we can be.

Losing a family member or a friend does not

mean that our lives are over. The person we lost was here with us for a reason. They gave meaning to our life and we gave their life meaning. They helped you become the person you are and they will continue to be a part of who you become in the future. Just because they are gone, does not mean that they will not affect your life. You may find yourself thinking in a few years about what they would say about something happening to you or wondering what they would do in a certain situation. It just gives us another reason to continue moving on. It gives us a purpose and the ability to live the way that we were meant to live.

As you are living your life, you need to have goals and you need to know how you are going to reach your goals. Why have goals if you are not going to do anything about them? Do you think that you can reach your goals withoutdoing something to move towards them? This is part of what makes you who you are. These goals are one of the reasons why you are here.

These are things that you can do that might help someone out, might save someone's life, you might make something that is useful. You should be spending each day planning and creating ideas of how you are going to reach your goals.

When you wake up each morning, look at your list of goals. Keep them right by your bed. Look at them and find one thing that you can do that day in order to get one step closer to your goals. Maybe it is making a new contact of who could be helpful in the future, or it could be making a few extra dollars that day so you can pay for what you need to reach that goal. Every small step counts and gets you that much closer to what you want.

Start talking to family and friends and see what they might be able to do to help you achieve your goals. Even though these are your goals, other people can give you information, so that you are successful. You should never turn away from information, unless of course it is something that is meant to destroy you. If someone does not want you to be happy, then they will do everything in their power to make sure that you do not succeed. Do not let this happen to you. You will want to be polite to these people, but do not let them deter you from your goals. Everyone has these people in their lives, but it is how you handle them that is important. Remember that your life is about you and what is important in to you. Everyone can have their own opinion, but they are not the ones living your life.Follow your heart and live your dreams.

I cannot stress this next one enough. Tell yourself that you are worthy each and every day. Tell yourself multiple times a day, especially if you are having a hard time believing it. You are worthy of your life. You are worthy of everything that has happened to you. Unfortunately, this includes all of the things that were not so good, but that is okay, you still earned them. Those things have made you into the person that you are today; the strong, dedicated, and intelligent person you have become. Your life is worth more than you can imagine.

All of the things we have spoken about so far are important and they are also what makes your life worth it. Your family, your friends, your coworkers and your neighbors make it worth it. Your children and grandchildren make every day worth it. Where would they be without you? Where would you be without them? These are very good questions to ask yourself when you are wondering if everything that you have done is worth it. Think about everything you have done so far in your life and where you might be if you had not had everything happen the way that it did.

Where would you be without your family? If you had listened to your teenage self and stopped speaking with your family, would you be where you are today? If you did not marry that special person in your life, would you be as happy as you are now? If you did not have those wonderful children, where would you be? This can also be true if you are divorced or if you suddenly lost a child or your parents died when you were young. Would you still be the same person you are today if that had not happened?

My guess would be that you would not. Your life would be different, because life is what you make of it. You choose the path that you want to take in life. We do not always choose the right one at the right time. We do not always choose the one that we need. However, we do make adjustments along the way, so we can be happy. We all realize as we continue on this adventure called life, that we are supposed to live for ourselves and that we are the only ones that can make us happy. We can try to make others happy as well, but it is their choice as to whether or not they will be happy. We cannot do anything to change how they feel.

We need to value ourselves and our lives, because if we don't, then we don't have anything. All of the money and physical items in the world will not be enough if we are not happy with our life. It will not be enough if we do not have what we truly want. The only things that we should really want in life are to be happy, have friends who mean something to us, have relationships that are special, and have family that we love. As long as we have all of those things, we should consider that we have everything that we need. The money and other items are nice, but not a necessity.

We should do our jobs and live our lives with the values that we have. If we value hard work, then we will do everything in our power to do our jobs properly. This can be rewarding to us, especially if we have a job where we help other people. If we can make others happy, because of what we are successful at, then we are doing something right. This should be the one time that we need to do our best to make someone else happy. This could be your purpose in life, so you need to be as successful as you can. Sometimes the best jobs that we can have are ones helping others.

Those who serve as nurses, doctors, social workers, and many other jobs, all do this on a daily basis. This is what everyone should be doing. Even if your job does not have you helping someone, you can find a way to do it. You can volunteer for a position where you are helping others. Giving back, even in a small way, can make you feel better and make you happier than you could ever imagine. If you are not sure what you could do, make some phone calls or talk to some friends. I am sure you can come up with something, even if it is just an hour a week. Go serve a meal to the homeless.

The smiles and the thank you's that you receive will be priceless. Donate items to the local food pantry. Volunteer for a local event in your town. These are all things that can be done and they do not take a lot of time or major commitment. They are all something that you can do, where you are helping others and yourself at the same time. Put yourself in other people's shoes. Would you want someone helping you out if you needed it? Of course you would. Try to help someone out when they need it.

Keeping a positive attitude is something that you have to try to do all of the time. I know that you may be thinking that it just is not possible, but you need to try. I am not suggesting you have the mindset of "I'm positive that I'm not going to do well." I am saying that you need to think that you are a good person, who is worth anything and everything and that you deserve the best. These are the thoughts that should be going through your mind. When you think good thoughts, good things can happen. These good things can even happen in bad situations. Think about how a new job you want to apply for can be better for you. Go into the interview saying that you know you are right for this position.

Go on the vacation of your dreams, with the thought that you are going to have the best time. Go to a restaurant or park and start a conversation with someone that you do not know. Keep that positive thinking going, because you don't know where you might meet that new best friend. Even if you're nervous and unsure of how things will go, the positive thinking will help you stay upbeat.

Besides, the worst that could happen is that you

won't get the job or have fun on the vacation or get a new best friend. Would that have changed if you thought negatively? Probably not. You would still get the same result.

However, by choosing positivity, you will not be as stressed or as worried in the situation that you are in. Not to mention that positive thinking is better for your health. We all know that stress is not good for anyone and additional stress will not change the outcome of any situation. If something bad happens, it is going to happen no matter what. Overthinking and creating more stress from it is not going to change the outcome. It will still happen. Let it go and move on with your life. Use whatever happens as a learning tool and keep going.

Everyone says that beauty is in the eye of the beholder. Why should the way you look at yourself be any different? You are the beholder and you need to know that you are beautiful inside and out.

Most people never believe that they look beautiful. Some people think we need to look like movie stars in order to get a date or anything else in life. Do you think that all movie stars think that they are beautiful? Nope, they do not, Not to mention, they have a whole team that makes them look picture perfect most of the time. I bet when they are hanging around their house, they are not looking picture perfect. They probably have no makeup on and their hair is not done, either. They probably put it up in a messy ponytail and call it a day, just like the rest of us.

You are the one who controls your life and how it turns out. YOU are the one who can make YOU happy. YOU are the one who can forgive yourself and forgive others. YOU are the one who can control your past and not let it get in the way of your future. YOU are the one who can find your purpose in life. YOU are the one who can live your life the way you want. YOU are the one who can never give up. YOU are the one who can do something every day in order to reach your goals. YOU are the one that can tell yourself that you are worthwhile every day. YOU are the one who can tell yourself that you are valuable every day. YOU are the one who can keep a positive attitude throughout life. YOU are the one that is in control of the beauty that you have. YOU are the one that can change how you are doing things.

Are YOU seeing a pattern here? Every one of these sentences has the word "YOU" in it. YOU are in charge. No one else has the ability to control your life. If there is someone in your life that is trying to control who you are and how you live, then that person probably should not be in your life.

If you had something bad happen to you when you were younger, that is not going to change what you can do with your life right now. It does not matter if it was the death of a parent or sibling, or money issues, or even the worst of them all, abuse. You can still be a happy, positive, loving, and giving person that has meaning. You can forgive everything that happened to you in the past and move on. Will it be easy? No, nothing is ever easy, but it can be done. You have the power to change the course of your life and learn from the past. Learn how you want to be treated and how you want to treat others. That is the beautiful thing about the past. If you do not like what happened, make sure it never happens again. Maybe that is your purpose in life. Maybe you should be helping others learn how to move on from their past. Maybe you should be showing others how they can change how they live.

Remember, it does not matter how your life started or how it continued until now. All that matters now is how you live your life now and in the future. Do you want to be the person that someone controls all of the time? Do you want to be the person that someone steps on because they can? Do you want to live your life being unhappy? I bet you want to be the one in control. You want to do what you want, when you want. You want to be the best person you can be! That can be true and it can happen. All you need to do is follow your heart, follow your dreams, and live your life!

If there is anything in your life that you are not

happy about, now is the time to change it. Think about what your life is like now. Are you happy with your job? Yes, great.! No. What would you rather be doing? Are you happy with where you live? If the answer is no, then where would you rather live? Would you like to move to another state or another area in the city you live in now? Take a chance and make the change. You may find that you are happier once you move. Are you single or are you married? Are you happy with that? How is your relationship with family and friends? Is it the best it can be? If you think it could be better, make the necessary changes so it can be!

Anything is possible if you believe in yourself. Believe in what you can do and what you can achieve. It may take time before you see the results of the changes you make. It may take time before you see the results in yourself, but you will notice them. Others will notice the changes. They will see how happy you are and how you are now living your life. They will tell you that they notice the changes too. It will make you feel better, knowing that the work you are doing for yourself is being noticed by others.

You should be proud of yourself for doing something for yourself. Not many people will take the initial step of wanting to be happier. It is a difficult choice to make and most people will decide that it is not worth it or that they cannot be bothered. You, however, decided you are worth it, You are worthwhile and deserve everything in life. You deserve to be happy and content and have everything that you need. Congratulate yourself for being the best YOU that YOU can be.

As you move towards your goals, you will have days when you feel like giving up. Maybe something does not work the way it should. Maybe you are not making progress as quickly as you would like. You have to make a decision for your future. You can either choose to move forward or backwards. Make a promise to yourself today that you will not give up. Here are five techniques that you can put into practice that will help you keep moving forward and prevent you from ever giving up:

1. Look at what you have accomplished so far. Although you may have set some pretty large goals, there are many small steps that needed to be taken. Stop and take stock of where you are now and where you started. You are no longer in the same place you were three months ago or even three weeks ago. Make sure to celebrate your wins along the way, even those small ones. Each small step leads you closer to where you want to be.

2. Keep your eyes on your goals, remembering why you chose those goals in the first place. When you set your goals, you had ideas of the rewards for meeting those goals. You visualized your life in light in that place of victory. Take some time to remember why you set those goals in the first place.

Visualize again the results and positive things you will have when you reach them.

3. Watch someone do something that seemed impossible or read an inspirational story. When you watch someone else do something seemingly impossible, your mind can relate to that victory. You can almost place yourself in their shoes. You can empathize with their feelings, realizing their victory with them. Just seeing someone else succeed can inspire you to want the same for yourself.

4. Set some smaller goals and accomplish them. When you become frustrated, with a very large goal looming in the future, think about some smaller goals you can meet on the way. There are always small tasks that can be accomplished that are still helping you on the way to your bigger goal. Remember to

celebrate meeting those smaller goals, and let them renew your commitment to your larger goal.

5. Take the word "quit" out of your vocabulary. Finally, do not let quitting be an option. If you completely remove it from your thought processes and your vocabulary, it ceases being an option. It is not even considered. You begin to think about all of the possibilities for accomplishing your goal, without even considering quitting. Make a promise to yourself to keep going! Do not quit! Keep your goals in the forefront of your mind, moving toward your goals each day, taking small steps and celebrating each victory. Remember the reason for setting your goals in the first place and remove the word 'quit' from your vocabulary. It is not an option. If you refuse to accept it, then you will

find yourself never giving up, especially on your most important mission: yourself.

You and I both have dreams. Both of us have hopes, wishes, and thoughts about whatwe want to accomplish in life. We ponder over it, reflect upon them, imagine, and wish they become a reality. If you give up, thinking it's too late, you're old, you don't have money, too busy to be dreaming, not ready, not smart enough, etc. you will never get there.

If you dream about it, fulfil it. Where there is a will there is a way. Set up goals and take one step at a time. It's never too late to start, whether you are 25 or 100. If you are passionate and enthusiastic about it, it has to come to you. Even if you fail, you have got to keep trying and rest assured from each attempt you make, you will learn, grow, and develop and that my dear friend will be your road to success.

Chapter 5

Promise to forgive often and to not hold grudges, never let your painful past dictate your future!

"Healing begins where the wound was made." - Alice Walker

"Living in the moment means letting go of the past and not waiting for the future. It means living your life consciously, aware that each moment you breathe is a gift." – Oprah Winfrey

What does it mean to forgive? Forgiveness is to stop feeling resentment or anger towards someone for an offense, false, or mistake that they may have made. Forgiveness is probably one of the most important, yet most difficult, things we can do. Forgiveness of yourself and others has important outcomes. Although it may seem like when we forgive, we are telling ourselves or another person that their actions are fine, it does not mean that. Rather, we are saying that we let go of the offense and are ready to move on with our lives.

You should never focus on failure. Errors happen, and you fail from time to time, but you have to be ready to step up again, and move ahead rather than losing everything just because you were torn down by a bit of bad luck. Occasional mishaps happen to all of us. The difference is in what you learn from your mistakes, and that will determine how you live your life today and in a future-oriented mode.

As a child, I can remember living with both my mom and dad, until one day my dad moved out. I was 10 years old when my father left and I can remember that day like it was yesterday. Why would my dad leave us? As a 10-year-old child I didn't quite understand or grasp why things were happening. I soon began to feel abandoned in my own home. It was the feeling of being at home with your family and loved ones, but still feeling alone or as if pieces are still missing to your puzzle. As is true of many daughters that fathers are our real life superheroes and we look up to them with a tremendous amount of respect. I had many thoughts running through my mind. "Does he love me? Did I do something wrong? Did my mom make him leave? What will happen to my family? How can we be a family without a father present?" These were the questions my young mind pondered upon. Even when I was given an answer, I still felt clueless and I continued to hold on to my level of abandonment as if it was my own personal issue, which later affected me in life.

Sometimes as children we take on more that we should, without even knowing it. Our parent's decisions affect us more than we think. Something that started as an agreed upon separation, translated to me feeling abandoned because I was born into a family that was being divided right in front of my eyes. What hurts the most is knowing that there is nothing that you can do about a decision your parents made. So why even carry that burden? I did.My relationship with my father weakened. We went from weekly visits to broken promises to no visits at all.

He was the first male figure that I looked up to that hurt me and made me sad. As all young daughters do, I never stopped loving him and I continued to arrange play dates with my dad, even though attempts were often unsuccessful. Because I was still a young daughter yearning for her father's attention and love, I could not help but try. As time went on, we grew further apart. I still loved him, but I did not seek his attention and love anymore. It became my new normal to not have a father around.

Even though I appeared to be moving forward past that issue in life, I took my abandonment issues into my adulthood and into my relationships. At times, I found myself building a wall around myself in order to protect myself from allowing people to get to know the real me. Other times, I would do whatever was necessary to keep my family together. In my relationships, I began to conform to what my mate wanted me to be instead of who I was. Living a life like this will cause you to lose your identity in a hurry. What I discovered when my parents separated, was that created a broken home for my sister and me. Even though my mom did the best she could do to raise us, there are still broken pieces to the puzzle that my sister and I never learned how to put together in this home. We were two young girls growing into women, searching for these missing pieces to our puzzle (whatever that may be) and not sure where to find them.

Throughout our childhood, our mom dated guys that were, in my opinion, not good replacements of my father or even good role models for that matter. As a result, my sister and I had to search for those missing pieces on our own, outside of our family. We did not get that positive role model figure in our home. We did not get the experience of a male perspective on learning and growing in life. The majority of the times, we are not handed all the necessary tools to achieve what we want out of life, we have to make way with the hands and family styles we are dealt.

As a teenager, I kept up the wall in effort to protect myself. Even though I was open to meeting new friends, my personal life was still a closed book. I controlled how close I would allow someone to be to me. My past fears became my future rejections because I was allowing past fears to control my level of determination to achieve future goals that I had set. I knew what I wanted out of life, but I would find an excuse or let fear hold me back from moving forward. It is important to analyze where we come from, when we begin searching for where we are going.

Oftentimes, if you get to the root of your life beginnings, you will unfold the hidden truths that reflect the person you are now. That closed book that I once was had a story behind it. From my childhood and well into adulthood, I tried to find those infamous missing pieces of my life. The road to finding those missing pieces consisted of bad decisions, painful relationships, life changing choices, and experiences that all make up the pieces to the woman I am today.

I never wanted to date forever. I had a goal of being a wife, even early on. My first love would appear to be the opposite of me, but I loved him with every ounce of my being. I was already book smart, so he introduced different street knowledge to me. It was a different relationship, but it sure did feel real. Even if he did not join me at school, he would always make sure I was there on time. He was a big supporter of my endeavors and all my high school functions I was involved in. Even when you love hard, it can become a dysfunctional relationship. This type of love made him and me separate into worlds of our own. We did not listen to our parents when they tried to control our relationship, creating a division between our moms and us. My mom did not approve of this relationship on any level, but we continued on in our own world.

Our first date almost ended in a nightmare. He had seen an enemy that he was in the middle of a rivalry with, and the group of guys he was with began chasing us in the car. We were speeding and then I heard shooting. I started screaming and fearing for my life. How could a first date consist of such violence? I remember asking him to take me home and he refused, stating that he knew I would not talk to him anymore if he took me home. He was probably right, so he kept me, asked for forgiveness and made me promises that he was going to change his lifestyle. I forgave and stayed with him. How did I fall for a drug dealer whose life consisted of the streets while mine consisted of more positive images of life? Despite his livelihood, he had a great heart and always kept a smile on my face.

We had our good and bad times and I can honestly say he loved me. Sometimes when someone does not treat you like you would have liked to be treated, you have to wonder whether a male ever taught him how to be a man, or was it the streets that he turned to for guidance and survival? I knew when I met him that I was more interested in his heart than I was in fixing his life flaws. I wore my heart on my sleeve, but because I was so infatuated with the term 'family,' I stayed strong by this boy. Nothing could separate us. I never knew why I chose the men I did, or even why I made many of my decisions in the past. Even early on I was a fixer, a 'let's help him change' type of woman. I thought I could help others more than myself, which later in life, I found out to be one of my biggest flaws. You cannot enter a relationship with a man having the mind frame that he will change because of you. I always wondered why damaged men were attracted to me. It was not until later on that I realized it was because I was a damaged woman. I yearned for that love from a male role that I missed from my father.

Since my life consisted of having an absent father and a lack of any positive male role model in life at the time, it made me want to create my own family as soon as possible. That yearning to fill that void created a space that made me make unclear decisions when it came to men and relationships. That void in my life caused me to lose my identity in relationships. I would push my goals and dreams to the side to help my boyfriend pursue his goals. I was 75% in the relationship and 25% into myself.

Let me point out that if this is you, then I suggest you ask yourself how you can allow someone to know the real you, if you hide and suppress your goals just to live for him? How is that fair to you or the relationship? It is important to know that a man cannot complete you. I repeat: A man cannot complete you. You have to be complete before you enter the relationship. You cannot value another person more than yourself. You have to be able to remain an individual, even though you are in a relationship. Promise yourself that you will not hide behind your significant others goals, life, and problems.

You are important as well and you deserve support and encouragement. It was not until a year or so later that my boyfriend went to jail and I received a scholarship to go away to college. He wanted me to stay local for college, but I wanted the college experienced and made the choice to leave. That decision put a damper on our relationship. I went off to school and we slowly but surely faded away. We often joked about those years later in life.

As you can see, out the gate, I migrated toward the first man who told me he loved me, no matter the lifestyle or the cost. I began attempting to fill a void in my life earlier on. A male telling me he loved me was my biggest requirement. Whenever you are faced with making life decisions and find yourself doing things as your brain is saying no, but your heart is saying yes, be careful. You could be creating your own painful beginnings. Have enough love for yourself to think clearly. You are, in most cases, your biggest competitor. You aim to please a hidden void,as a result, you have neglected every other part of your existence. If you were like me, you do not know your worth or your true value. I was only 15, but due to the abandonment I had felt as a child, I made adult decisions to complete my newfound family. I lived this life because this is what I thought was required of me to hold my family down.

It is okay to have made those mistakes, because we made the best decisions we could at the time, based on the only experiences we had. One thing about life is that it does not come with instructions, which is why it is okay to make mistakes. Mistakes are the blue print to the design of our life plan. We have to be clear about what we want out of life, so that life can be clear on what to give us. How do we even begin to get there?

Years later, I found myself in another serious relationship, my first real relationship as an adult. I met a guy who appeared to be a caring, successful, and a family man. I thought for sure he loved me more than I loved him. What I ended up in was a very controlling relationship that caused me to lose myself. He never hit me, but he controlled my mind, which, to me, is a much more powerful form of control. He never let me leave his side to do extracurricular activities with friends or even have a job, for that matter. I believe he thought I was his property. I stayed in this relationship and conformed because I thought his controlling nature was a sincere level of love he had for me.

Even though I felt like I was walking on egg shells in this relationship, I stayed in order to work towards this family I always envisioned. As 2 years , it became clear that this was a love that I did not want to be a part of. I was scared that one day his controlling nature could change to a more violent nature. If I missed his calls, there was a problem. If I stayed inside the grocery store too long, there was a problem. Even if I came home 10 minutes late from class, it was a problem. I was 1,000 miles away from my home state and any family members, so I often sat and wondered, "Is this the life, or the family that I was so eager to be in?"

He was all I knew and all I had as family, since I moved away to school. As his controlling nature grew, I soon began to feel more scared. I can remember us going to my friend's party together. As I entered the party, I saw a few of my male classmates, so I stopped to speak and my boyfriend completely snapped and yelled aloud, telling me that we had to go (even though we had just gotten there). He yelled and screamed at me the whole ride home. He was so upset that he drove 90 miles an hour on the back country roads to our apartment.

I was afraid he was going to crash and end my life. He swerved the car off the road and almost hit a pole, but he hit the brake seconds before. The next scene in this relationship would forever be life-changing for me. I found out that I was pregnant. Even though I was in a relationship, this was one of the loneliest moments of my life. There I was, pregnant, which was one of the scariest and most nerve wrecking experiences I had ever encountered. When I first told him the news, he reacted as if we would not be able to enjoy life anymore if we let a baby come into this world. I was so shocked at his response. Of course we were both young, but I felt that we should also be responsible for our actions. He thought otherwise. I remembered thinking, "How could the person that I chose to have a baby with love me more than the baby itself?" He felt we should get an abortion so that we could still enjoy our relationship, and initially I agreed.

I remember us driving to the abortion clinic and seeing all those anti-abortion protesters outside. I could not believe we drove this far to kill our unborn baby. We both walked inside to the counter and the cashier reminded us that there is no refund after this point. He paid the cashier and we sat down, waiting for them to call my name.

Those were the longest 15 minutes of my life; every thought went through my head. I looked toward him and told him that I could not do it just before standing up and walking towards the door to leave. He was mad because he felt that our traveling sprees and carefree lives were over. From that day forward, he made life harder and harder for me, which put so much stress on the baby and myself. Something that I thought would be a great, but nervous experience, consequently led me to choosing between my child and my relationship.

As a result, I decided the relationship was not healthy and that I was tired of hiding behind my fears. That decision meant I had to raise my child on my own. Even though it has been hard, I still believe I made the right decision, despite the consequences of having to be a single mom. In the end, I am happy about the choice I made to give my baby life.

Whenever you are faced with a life changing experience, make sure you choose solutions based on your own needs first. Never make a decision based on someone else's life, especially when you will be impacted by the result as well. Even years later, he holds a grudge with me for leaving him. I suppose he is still trying to punish me by not building a relationship with our child. This relationship hurt me beyond measure, because it also affected our child and still does. I tried to make amends for the sake of our child, so we could at least be cordial parents, but he is still trying to punish me for taking a stand in our relationship, since I moved on and did not want to be controlled any more. So what do you do when you have a child by a person and they still holding a grudge? When they are not in the child's life actively and you are left to parent your child on your own? It is a sad but true reality for a lot of us. My biggest fear had come true again; I am a single mother, raising a child without any involvement from their father.

This was the hardest pill to swallow. I already had no idea how to be a mother, now on top of that, I would have to support and raise the baby by myself. How did I keep finding myself in these broken relationships? Why me? When you find yourself in situations you cannot control, seek spiritual guidance. What part of your puzzle is missing? What part did you play in the painful situation? Be clear as to what you will and will not accept when you enter a new relationship. This task will help you when the time comes to giving your heart away. We often overlook many of the signs, when we are dating. You have to be honest with yourself and realize that if it hurt in the beginning, then there is a good chance that it will hurt more in the end. Do not overlook the signs and make excuses for someone's behavior.

If you are finding that you are always thinking of your past, you will need to do something to change that. I am not talking about all of those happy thoughts that you keep going back to. Those thoughts are perfect. Those are the thoughts that will keep you going in the future. Those are the thoughts that will bring back wonderful memories of people and times you love and cherish. I am talking about the thoughts of when you were not happy, when you screwed up somewhere, or you fought with someone, etc. You cannot continue with your life if you keep bringing the past back in. The past is the past and there is nothing that you can do to change it.

For years I resented the father of my child and my own father, because I felt that same abandonment as I did when I was ten years old. For the next coming years after my child was born, I carried that pain, resentment, disappointment, and frustration with me. It became who I was, and as you know, hurt people hurt other people. I began attracting who I was at the time. One day, when I was reflecting on my life, I started crying. I knew something was not right in my life. I felt I took a complete U-turn from where I imagined I would be. I felt myself starting to become depressed and all alone.

My days soon began to be filled with tears of hurt and confusion. I did not know where to go or where to find answers. I began to search for my truths, because only that can set me free. As I searched for clarity, I had that famous "ah ha!" moment. All these years, I had been carrying this burden and being an involuntary victim of my own life. I decided I had to forgive, even if he never apologized. Forgiving him does not mean that I am weak. Forgiving him showed how strong I was to forgive someone who never even apologized.

Sometimes in life, we have to make executive decisions to make ourselves our own priority. I had to do that in order to set myself free from his bondage. Even though I felt he was wrong in his actions, I could not live in that moment of pain for the rest of my life. I was allowing him to write pages in my life story that I was supposed to be the only author of. I cannot be a victim in my own life; I cannot worry or carry depression over things that I have no control over. I will no longer point the fingers at other people's actions.

I will own up to the part I played in my life story. Ownership is just the beginning, but join me on this mission, as I attempt to put the missing pieces of this life of mine- my own puzzle- together. There are five reasons to forgive yourself and others to make a real difference in your life:

1. **Forgiveness** of yourself helps you to move on. You will never benefit from guilt. It brings you down and keeps you from accomplishing the most important things in life. Stated simply, you cannot change the past. However, if you do not forgive and let go, you will not be able to move into the future.

2. **Forgiveness** is an act of strength. It is easy to hold onto a grudge, stay angry and play the offense overin your mind. However, it takes great strength to forgive, but it is even harder to forget. Like building muscles, it gets easier each time as you grow stronger in yourself and in your relationships. "The weak can never forgive. Forgiveness is the attribute of the strong." ~Ghandi

3. **Forgiveness** is something that you must do for yourself. It might sound like the offender will benefit from your forgiveness, but the truth is, you are the one who is angry and hurt. Once you decide to forgive, you are letting yourself off the hook, so to speak. You find that you have no reason to be hurt and angry. The offense is forgotten. The hurt is no longer and before long, you will not remember the reason you were angry. As you forgive, you give yourself the gift of healing.

4. **Forgiveness** results in peace within yourself and with others. As you forgive, you find that you are no longer hurt and angry, and you begin to heal. This healing results in an inner peace. As you forgive yourself and others, you no longer carry a grudge. It is almost as though forgiveness leaves a hole in your heart, where hurt and anger use to reside and this hole is filled with peace, joy and happiness.

5. **Forgiveness** gives you the opportunity to move on with your life and live life to the fullest. As long as you carry hurt, anger, or remorse you are held bound by these feelings. However, the moment you decide to forgive yourself and others. You demonstrate your strength to let go of the past and move on with your life. You let go of the baggage

you are carrying and move forward, free of hurt, anger, guilt and blame.

If you want to live a life of happiness, you must make a promise to yourself to forgive yourself and others. As long as you are carrying the baggage of hurt, you cannot move forward. It is time to let go of the past and look forward to a life of happiness.

Forgiveness, the forgiveness of others and forgiveness of self, is essential if you are to progress spiritually and reunite with your true and higher self. Non-forgiveness binds you energetically to the other person and your lower self and ego. Along life's path we all encounter situations that hurt us and cause us pain. It can be difficult, or seemingly impossible, to forgive the ones who have caused us such pain or committed heinous acts against us.

Many of these situations strongly engage our emotions and energies, which in turn creates an energy matrix and pattern. Although unseen, these matrices are every bit as real as any physical object on earth and will stay intact until the situation is resolved or the energies are transmuted. This locks some of your energy in the past, many times to your own detriment. The past is dead and gone, and yet the past is kept "alive" by non-resolution of the matter. At best, it sits there and festers.

If you continue to bring up these situations and go overthem in your mind, you feed the energy matrix and cause it to grow stronger. By the Universal Law of Attraction, this in turn attracts like energy to you based on what you are outputting emotionally concerning the incident. If you are angry, anger returns to you, multiplying and fueling the original energy output. This energy can affect you on the physical, emotional and mental levels. The non-resolution of the issue continues to link you to the situation and binds you to any others involved through karma until the situation is resolved - in this lifetime or another.

NOTE: Until you truly forgive someone or

something, you are bound to that situation or person. Forgiveness of self may be the most difficult of all. The other aspect of forgiveness, the forgiveness of oneself, can prove to be the most difficult of all. We can be our own worst enemies, going over all our misdeeds and wrongs we have committed. Many times as a result of the non-forgiveness of self, you subconsciously end up sabotaging things in your life as punishment. This is why it is essential to include forgiveness of self, along with forgiving others.

Forgive and Forget?

Sometimes we are told we must "forgive and forget." In truly forgiving someone or something, you do not forget the incident, that would be impossible. However, you do let it go. Realize that you don't have to "forgive and forget". You can still acknowledge that you or someone else did something wrong while at the same time forgiving.

Many times, the ego wants the other to be

punished or see justice prevail before truly forgiving and letting go. Knowing and understanding the Law of Karma (also known as the Law of Cause and Effect) is helpful in letting go. It states that for every action there will be an equal and opposite reaction; which means that if you give happiness, you will receive happiness in return and if you give sorrow, you will receive sorrow in return. In other words, "as you sow, so shall you reap".

The Law of Karma is indisputable and unerring. Thus you may know that Divine Justice will prevail. Knowing this, do not worry about things out of your control and simply handle whatever you can change because the world is conspiring to help you.

CHAPTER 6

Promise to keep a positive attitude and surround yourself around positive people.

"Give light and people will find the way"~~ Ella Baker

In life we come across people, friends, relationships, coworkers and partnerships for a reason. I do not believe meeting people is an accident. Whether they stay in your life for a season or a lifetime, it is all for a reason. It is important to understand the lesson or reason in order to learn from the experience. One thing about relationships is that sometimes they can be predictable, but oftentimes, they can come with some unsuspected life lessons called obstacles.

As you can recall from the first chapter, I was a

reserved person, so I kept a few close friends, but I had tons of associates. I did not understand why I only kept a few close friends in the past, but I do now. Let me explain my journey.

This promise took me some years to understand, because, as you can remember, I always entered relationships with the attitude of, "Don't worry about little old me. Let's work on your goals and bring your vision to life. we can work on my goals later." That attitude can drain you fast. If you keep withdrawing all your knowledge and love and putting it into someone else's knowledge bank, then you will end up depleted and in complete bankruptcy status. You have to be in a situation where knowledge and support is being poured back into you as well. That is why boundaries are so important. If you do not set boundaries for yourself, you could end up in a one-sided relationship, going down a one-way street, with one set of goals being accomplished and it will not be yours.

Keeping a positive attitude can help you meet

your goals, and be happier. Although we are constantly bombarded by negativity in our minds and our environment, it is important to make a promise to yourself to maintain a positive attitude every day. The following are five ways that can help you keep a positive attitude and rebuke negativity:

1. Practice positive affirmations daily. Remember those positive affirmations, those wonderful little things about you that you love. Speak those to yourself every day. Look in the mirror and give yourself a pep talk, reminding yourself of all those qualities that make you beautiful and unique.

2. Keep negative thoughts away. Research says that 80% of our daily thoughts are negative. Get rid of them. Try the rubber band trick. Place a rubber band on your wrist and every time a negative thought enters your mind, pop the rubber band to remind you to

replace that thought with a positive one. Stay away from the negative things around you- negative people, the news, negative stories. Fill your life with positive thoughts, and keep the negative ones away.

3. Maintain focus on your goals and your future. If you allow it, it can be easy to let yourself become frustrated by circumstances or hindrances to your goals. Remember to stay focused on your goals and the future you are building for yourself. Do not become distracted by the annoyances of the day or even the seemingly insurmountable obstacles. Instead, visualize the future and meeting your goals. Do it daily to maintain your focus and your positive attitude.

4. Watch your words. Your words can either make you or break you. When you speak negativity, your brain recognizes those

thoughts as reality. Instead, make a decision, today, to only let positive words leave your mouth. Each time you speak positively, your brain recognizes those words, too. They make a difference in your thought processes. While you are at it, make sure everyone around you is speaking positively as well. If they are not, you may need to go somewhere else.

5. Keep an attitude of gratitude. Finally, keep in mind all the wonderful things about your life. You are a strong, beautiful person with a wealth of gifts. List those things that are wonderful about your life, and keep them at the forefront of your mind. When you keep in mind that you have so many things for which you can be thankful, the negativity remains at bay.

Make a promise to yourself, today, that you will maintain a positive attitude, keeping an eye on your thoughts and your words. Maintain your focus on your goals and the wonderful things that make you the strong, beautiful person that you are. Then, remember to be thankful! It is important to always be your biggest fan, do not give that position to anyone but yourself. You have to affirm to yourself daily that you are worthy of all great things that life has to offer.

In the past when I woke up, I immediately wanted to go back to bed. Even if I got at least 8 hours of sleep, I still did not have the drive to face the world. Something was weighing me down and was not allowing me to face it. I started to wake up each morning and look in the mirror and speak positive affirmations to myself. I notice that we often tell ourselves negative things each day, which is probably what is weighing us down. So why not tell ourselves something positive and change perspective on our life? It is okay to have a voice and high self-esteem. You deserve everything your significant other deserves. Practice saying you are worthy in the mirror. We have to be our biggest supporter first, before we can expect someone else to be one.

One of my personal daily affirmations that I wrote to tell myself was "I believe in all things positive, let my blessings flow from inside and out. My faith is my leader and I will always remain true to myself. Miracles are possible and love is real, my vision will remain clear and my purpose is the way I shall live!" This is my personal message to myself every day. It is imperative and critical to be your biggest supporter through your life journey.

Throughout life, I battled with the thoughts that I was not good enough, in shape enough, pretty enough or successful enough. I learned we are our biggest critics and if we do not support ourselves first, then we have lost the battle on life already. I remember after having my first child, my weight and body shape became an issue for me. I was not the biggest fan of exercising, or even eating healthy, for that matter. I had come to a point in my life where I had to start standing for something and that something just had to be me for a change.

When you wake up in the morning and look in the mirror and are not happy with what you see, that is a problem. We have to love who we are even amongst the storm. We have to give ourselves the benefit of the doubt that we are worthy and that we all have a divine purpose. It is our job to find our purpose and live in it. There is just no other option. Do not second guess your worth. It is mandatory to love yourself first or, no one else will.

Look at it like this- how many times have you worked toward something and failed? Well guess what? Failure is all a part of life and it is better to have tried and failed then to have not tried at all. Unfortunately, if you avoid failure, then you will avoid success. How would you know your strengths or weaknesses if you did not try and attempt to accomplish goals in life? Our strengths help us determine our boundaries that we set and that we use to measure throughout life. So let us not limit ourselves or put our extraordinary selves in a small or narrow box. We were designed to shine bright like the little diamonds that we are.

For example, have you ever had a great idea or plan and started working towards accomplishing it? Then here comes Jo Blow, who might come in the form of a family member or a friend who throws another idea out there that they feel you should do and they give you reasons as to why you should not do the idea that you were working toward. And what do you know? You believe him or her and switch your goals around because of that one conversation. That is all it takes. One simple conversation can have you chasing someone else's vision. That is why it is important to live with a purpose, so every decision you make somehow connects to your purpose.

Life can be merciless. There is so much competition for jobs, it is difficult to find (and keep) compatible friends and lovers, and health can be fleeting. There are victories, but there are also failures. People find romance, but they also lose it every day. Good-paying employment can be difficult to secure. Also, while good health is fantastic, most of us take it for granted, and health can be gone in a flash.

That is why it is so important to surround yourself with positive people. In fact, surrounding yourself with positive, supportive people who do not begrudge your successes, who encourage you to be accountable for your own actions, who motivate you to be the best you can be, and who support you when things get tough, is one of the most important things that you can do for yourself. Life is hard enough – can you imagine it without your closest friends?

Friends are the people who get us through our rough days, who listen and bring us ice cream when we have been dumped (again), and who will listen to us rant about our bosses and our workload. They sometimes help us come up with solutions to our problems, but even when they do not have ideas or advice to give us, they are content to just listen and sympathize. We feel better after talking with our friends, and ready to go out and face the world again.

In return, we support our friends when they need us. These reciprocal relationships are one of the most important of our lives. Often, these friends become our extended family. However, there is also the term of having people in your life that are draining you and causing you more harm than good. If 90% of the time a friend causes you pain, brings negativity or discomfort, unfortunately it is time to move on.

Years of friendship is great, but there is no compromise when people's lives consume you more than they consume them. I had friends in my life, I had to make the executive decision to take the good with the bad, but I had no choice but to walk away. Even if you express the issues that you have with them and months or years pass, you have to love them from a distance because you don't have any more room for them, because you are drained and depleted and the friendship is taking a toll. Boundaries are important with friendships as well.

There is no doubt in my mind that surrounding yourself with positive people will impact your results in life. Wasting so much time trying to change the perspective of negative people usually ends up without any success.

3 important rules happy people usually live by:

- They appreciate what they have
- They appreciate potential
- They always look ahead instead of living in the past

Let's go through these points so you can also get the full potential from living by these rules. These are essential identifying signs on who is worth your attention when you want to build up mutually beneficial relationships, and when you want to identify what works - and what does not work.

Appreciating What You Have

Happy people appreciate the gifts they have received. Whether it is talent for helping others, or a talent for instruction, writing or speaking, these gifts will always be focused on helping others. Their entire perspective is centered around building up rather than tearing down.

When you see people who do not appreciate their talents, you need to get focusedagain. You can't work with them until they are ready to build on a solid foundation. People who can't identify their foundation will be building on quicksand, and can never get motivated to stick with the assignment at hand.

Appreciating Potential In Yourself and

People Around You

Rather than being envious, you should be glad when you are around people who grow even faster than yourself. It just proves your methods work. Learning curves are different for all people, and growth comes in periodic steps. Sometimes we stand still, yet suddenly a border is passed, and then growth speeds up for some time. When growth slows down people need restructuring, and perhaps even a changed focus to help keep them ready for more growth in the future. You are capable of constantly building on yourself and who you are in order to reach where you want to be. Like a plant that grows toward the sun, aim upwards towards brighter things.

Chapter 7

Promise to OWN your beauty and remain true to yourself!

"Self Esteem means knowing you are the dream".
~~Oprah Winfrey

A lack of self-worth is one of the main causes of us, either allowing controllable things to happen to us, or doing negative things to other people. Either way, we are lacking something, as a result. If you are not your biggest supporter, then you cannot expect anyone else to be. Do not waste time convincing people to support you and your goals. Just use that time to better your craft. If someone asked you to describe yourself in one word, what would you say?

Who are you? Behind closed doors, when the storm is putting on pressure, who are you then? Be clear on your answers, because knowing your true authentic self is key to discovering your true self worth.

What is beauty? We are constantly bombarded with pictures, ads, and ideas about beauty. Society says beauty is thin and young, but the truth is that we are all beautiful. No matter what size, shape, or color, we each have something about us that makes us different and unique, something that makes us stand out from the crowd. You have the power to define beauty, because you are beauty. Now, you have to own it.

The key to being beautiful is owning it. Know who you are and accept who you are. Love yourself with all of your flaws and blemishes, the quirkiness, and the loveliness. Take pleasure in knowing who you are, what you believe, and reaching your goals. Be deliberate in setting the stage with enthusiasm for your next step and satisfaction with yourself. Let that light shine in the world, sharing your beauty with others.

Your thoughts and opinions about your looks, gifts, and characteristics play the greatest part of owning your beauty and staying true to your authentic self. These thoughts and opinions make up your self-esteem. Your self-esteem is your overall emotional evaluation of your true self and your worth. It is the way you judge yourself, and the value that you place on yourself. Self-esteem can be high or low, and either can cause long-lasting effects on your decisions, your goals, and your life.

At some point in our lives, each and every one of us has felt insecure, unworthy, unattractive, incompetent, or some other form of inadequacy. In fact, studies have shown that 85% of us feel that way more often than not. This is called low self-esteem and it stems from a multitude of things; the societal view of success or beauty, traumatic experiences, disapproving authority figures, bullying from your peers, etc. While low self-esteem is not a recognized health problem, it can be just as debilitating and can keep you from living the life you deserve.

Low self-esteem can hinder our ability to reach the goals we set for ourselves. It can hinder us from realizing our inner beauty. It can cause us to make self-destructive decisions under the pretense that we do not deserve better. A woman may stay in an abusive relationship because of low self-esteem, telling herself that no one else will ever love her. A teenage girl may develop an eating disorder because a group of girls told her she was fat or a television commercial told her being thin was important. A teenage boy may start indulging in drugs because an abusive parent once told him he was worthless.

In many cases, low self-esteem can be the root of anxiety and depression. It can cause a person to be anxious in social situations, always looking for signs that others are noticing their self-perceived inadequacy. When these feelings of worthlessness fester for long enough, a person may then decide to avoid social situations all around. They may lay in bed more frequently, telling themselves that they have no reason to get up and breathe the air of the people who are adding something to the world.

"Self-esteem attacks," much like anxiety attacks, occur when a person says or does something that they later deem to have been stupid, inappropriate, or embarrassing. They may experience extreme anxiety, a racing heart, and will berate himself for minutes, hours and in extreme cases, days.

Keeping healthy relationships with others can be nearly impossible if you suffer from low self-esteem. A person with low self-esteem may be overly focused on themselves, constantly seeking approval and become defensive if they don't receive it. This type of person may indulge in whatever satisfies their need to feel more complete, never taking into consideration the feelings of others. It would obviously be difficult to maintain a healthy, honest relationship with a person who needs to constantly be reminded that they are loved. Their self-worth is dependent upon the opinions of those around them.

Conversely, a person with high self-esteem knows who they are, what they believe, and what they want. They recognize their inner beauty and own it. They do not look to others for approval because they approve of themselves, knowing they are beautiful and strong and in control of their destiny. Relationships are fulfilling because friends, family, and significant others add to their lives, rather than define who they are. Powerful decisions are made as they see the truth and act accordingly. Most importantly, a person with high self-esteem can look at themselves in the mirror, see who they are, and love themselves.

It is clear that low self-esteem can greatly decrease our quality of life, while on the other hand, maintaining a positive self-esteem allows us to learn and grow from our mistakes without the fear of rejection. A positive outlook on yourself will help, rather than hinder, your ability to set and reach goals. Think about all of those people who made unhealthy decisions because of their low self-esteems: the woman in the abusive relationship, the teenage girl suffering from an eating disorder, and the teenage boy who used drugs to numb his self-loathing. What if these people had realized their worth?

Our self-esteem is a direct reflection of the quality of our relationships with other people. A person with a high self-esteem does not seek approval and praise from those around them. tThey are endowed with the ability to give rather than take. They are able to give respect, love, and attention, not only to their loved ones, but also to themselves.

Maintaining a high self-esteem is imperative in order to live a positive, fulfilling life. The question, now, is 'how do we go about building this magical life-changing self-esteem?' Here are the five most important steps you must take in order to boost your self-worth and break the chains of poor self-esteem. Positive self-esteem stems from knowing who you are. The world is constantly telling us who we ought to be, but who are you? This is not a question that can be answered with a name or a social security number and many people would answer this question with "I'm a mom," or "I'm a teacher." Try to keep in mind that what you do does not define who you are as a person. Now, with this in mind, take a look at yourself: your appearance, your beliefs, your morals and ethics, your talents and passions, your priorities etc. Decide on the things you like about yourself. Think about what makes you unique and sets you apart from your peers. Think about the things you are good at and the achievements you have made. Write down all of the qualities that make you proud to be you, as little or as many as that may be. (You will need this list for the next step.) A well–known author was quoted as saying that "The average person has 60,000 thoughts per day and of these more than 80% are negative." Negative self-talk is probably the quickest way to a low self-esteem.

One of the most effective ways to combat low self-esteem is the use of affirmations. First, grab the list you made in step one and a pretty piece of paper. Using the following format, use your list to create your affirmation statement.

"I am beautiful, both inside and out.

I am talented.

I am strong.

I am not what they say I am."

Try adding things you would like to see happen in your life.

"I will be kind to everyone I come in contact with.

" I will take care of my body by eating right and exercising regularly."

Once you have created your perfect statement, take it and tape it to the mirror in your batrhroom. Every morning when you get up to brush your teeth, read off your affirmations to yourself, out loud. Positive self-talk is an incredibly important approach in maintaining a positive attitude and building your self-esteem. These activities may seem silly or embarrassing at first, but reaffirming yourself out loud every day plants a seed in your mind that will eventually blossom into a beautiful, healthy self-esteem.

1.Take Care of Yourself

When you avoid doing the things that cause you to feel mentally and physically well, you deprive yourself of the confidence that comes along with them. Taking time out of your day to practice self-care is essential and there are a multitude of things you can do that will boost your morale.

It has been said that when you look your best, you feel your best. Maybe you have been slacking on your appearance for whatever reason: a busy schedule, a lack of motivation, or a stressful situation, but paying a more attention to the way you look will boost your confidence and allow you to feel more secure during social interactions. Spend more time putting on your makeup or try out a new hair color. Treat yourself to a manicure or buy yourself a new outfit. (These days, even men are likely to be found in a nail salon.)

A healthy body leads to a healthy mind. Eating right and exercising releases dopamine in the brain, causing you to feel happier, be more energized, and sleep better. Even something as simple as taking your dog out for a short walk two or three times a week or choosing a glass of water over a soda can make a world of difference.

2. Stop Comparing Yourself to Others

As humans, we instinctually compare ourselves to those around us, causing us to feel inadequate tothose who have more money, seem more attractive, are more successful etc. Not only does it cause us to feel like lesser of a person, but it also makes us forget to appreciate the things that make our lives wonderful. This way of thinking is destructive and represents a battle that can never be won. No matter how much you have, there will always be someone who has more. Conscientiously realizing this is an important step in getting a handle on this useless routine.

The habit of comparing yourself to others can easily be replaced with a healthier, more productive habit, comparing yourself to yourself. This small shift in thought instigates attitudes of appreciation and self-approval by allowing us to reflect on how much we have grown as people, the achievements we have made, and the people we have met along the way. Keep this trick handy so that, when you are tempted to compare yourself to someone else, you can, instead, compare yourself to yourself.

3. Live as Your Most Authentic Self

Most of us, throughout our lives, have molded a mask or a "fictional self" with which to interact with the world. We do this subconsciously, of course, because we know how much easier it is to simply fill the roles expected of you by your family, friends, and society, rather than rock the boat or stir up conflict. Because we have spent so much of our lives interacting through our fictional selves, we have neglected our authentic selves, causing them to fade into the background. Living life through your fictional self will leave you feeling empty and unfulfilled, as a result ofdoing and being what the world has told you that you should do and be. Your fictional self acts as a firewall, keeping out the information necessary for staying in touch with your authentic self.

Your authentic identity cannot be identified by your career, your bloodline, or your function in relation to society. It is everything you are at your core. It is the wisdom you have gained from all of your life experiences, and the unique traits and talents you were born with. It is the person you were created to be.

A healthy self-esteem has to be built upon your most authentic self, or else it is a façade, built upon the person the world has told you to be rather than the person you really are. If you are living as your authentic self, you know who you are and what makes you unique. You refuse to be defined by your weight, your IQ score, the size of your house, or the opinions of others. You define yourself and you are not afraid to be different, quirky, or even downright weird. You know when and how to say no and you do things for people because you want to, not because you are expected to. Self-esteem is one of the most important things in our lives. Self-esteem can make or break our decisions, our relationships with ourselves and others, and can become the ultimate factor in deciding whether we reach our goals.

Just as the key to owning your beauty is self-esteem, the key to a healthy self-esteem is owning your beauty. You define beauty and it is up to you to show your beauty to the world. Grab hold of those things you love about yourself, maybe even the things you do not, and own them. Remind yourself daily of how great you are. Remind yourself that you are beautiful, strong, and in control of your destiny. Take time to take care of yourself, nurturing your mind, body, and spirit. Be true to yourself, knowing there is no one else in the world like you. Lastly, be authentic. Show the world your true greatness, for you are the author of your life story and your story is one worth telling. It is the greatest action, adventure, romance, mystery novel that you will ever know, and it is entirely yours to own and show the world.

Chapter 8

Promise to Remain the Author in your LifeStory and Be the Change that You Want to See!

"Stepping onto a brand-new path is difficult, but not more difficult than remaining in a situation, which is not nurturing to the whole woman."
— Maya Angelou

Where do you go when you want to see results? Your local congressman, president, police station, or committee office? While those are good places to go for change, you ultimately need to start with yourself. You have to ask yourself what you can do to bring about the change you need and why it is important for this change to even happen. When you look in the mirror you are looking at the biggest change agent that you know. From the moment we are born, each of us has an individual path that we take. It is like no one else's. When we run into life's challenges and obstacles, we are the ones that are best equipped to help ourselves through that rough spot. Think about it. Others can motivate you, and mentor you, but nobody can help you the way you can help yourself. You know what your limits, are, what your strengths are, and what you want out of life and what you can and cannot tolerate.

What can you do when life hands you a dilemma? Look inside yourself for inspiration. First of all, this requires knowing yourself. Ask yourself what your life purpose, or life's goal are. Any decision you make should have the end result of supporting that particular goal. Second, you need to believe in yourself. When you believe that you can do something, that confidence will keep you moving forward. Confidence will give you the courage to forge ahead and keep working towards your goal. What happens when you do not have the confidence? You start questioning yourself about whether you made the right decision, and might start talking yourself into giving up.

To achieve life's goals and overcome the many obstacles associated with living, you need to love and be there for yourself. Be your own cheerleader and motivator, and feel the power come from within. Why is being the author of your life important? Why would you want to give someone full control over your destiny? You hold the pen, so make sure each day you write a new page to your life book. Whatever your heart desires, you should aim and reach towards those goals. Nobody is responsible for your life, but you. The key to open your future doors are in the palm of your hands. What is change? Why do we fear it? Change is to cause to be different from what something used to be. When we decide to change something about ourselves, we are taking steps towards becoming or making our situations different from what they are currently.

There are many ways to overcome fear and be the change you want to see. Fear is the word that we sometimes give too much power. Some of the things we fear can can push us toward toward better things to come. Embrace change, face your fears, and work towards what you feel you deserve in life. You cannot allow fear to win, because you might regret the unknown or just become accustom with remaining content with settling for what life gives you, instead of what you are worth.

Fight for your worth and do not settle for less. We deserve all of what life has to give, we need to focus on doing things that make us happy, and this promise to yourself cannot be compromised. Do not let things that do not make you happy stress you out. Some things we cannot change from happening, but we can definitely change how we react to it. Do not let negativity live in your heart or mind.

Always live your life out of a place of peace and love. Love has been the cause for relationships mending and people succeeding in life. Use love to your advantage and worth through unconditional, loyalty and courage. Make sure you promise to know your purpose, so you do not continue to go through this world without a vision or plan to succeed. The quickest way to depression is living without purpose, so this is a critical promise to keep to yourself.

Throughout life there will be obstacles The most successful people will tell you to never give up. No matter how many times you fall, or how many times people, jobs, or banks tell you no, keep going because there is light at the end of the tunnel that will guide you to where you want to go. Keep Going!

Remember to be clear on what you want out of life, so that life can be clear on what to give you"! ~

TJ Freeman

__About the Author__

"There was always something acting as a push throughout my life. It was not destiny and I never credit my fate for taking me where I am right now. It has always been by courage to challenge the certainty. I worked on faith a lot of times to stay strong, while I faced obstacles in my personal and professional life.

My courage and consistency has got me to that point I am at today. Each day it's all about getting to know yourself better and learning what is necessary to work in your purpose.Struggles and adversity has always been a part of my journey, but my will and strength to surpass my expectations has caused me to stay focused and turn the wheel back on the road to success when I find my self-steering off" ~TJ Freeman

Author TJ Freeman is the CEO of Promising Purpose LLC, which is a Life Coaching and Smal Book Publishing Company. She is a Life and Confidence Coach, Educator, Speaker, Author and Founder of a nonprofit called TJ Promise Kids. She is the mother of two beautiful children and currently in graduate school to receive her Master's Degree. Despite her past issues of abandonment, painful relationships and becoming a single parent mother, she decided to create life opportunities, instead of letting her past dictate her future and letting life past her by.

She began to build confidence within herself to find her purpose, follow her dreams and help others along the journey. She soon began to learn how to face her obstacles with a different perspective and learn that life is what you make it. She devoted herself to helping others, so that others who have experienced those same obstacles could learn to overcome and take back their life, no matter the storm.

She started out by helping at risk youth, through her nonprofit TJ Promise Kids. TJ was inspired to create TJ Promise Kids based on her first-hand experience as an Abuse Advocate for the Juvenile Court System. There she learned how to help children overcome life's obstacles and reach new heights. Her mission is to be a voice for at risk youth. She led community based workshops on violence, relationships, self-esteem, overcoming obstacles, and more. Now she is working with adults, helping them overcome obstacles and reach their next desired level in life. She has written her first motivational book titled "Life the Way I Know it" 8 Promises to Live By, where she gives her interpretation of her life experiences and how she turned her breakdowns into breakthroughs. She gives 8 promises that you should promise to ourselves, so we can aim for our true potential, discover our life purpose and take charge of our life in a happier, purposeful and successful way.

www.ingramcontent.com/pod-product-compliance
Lightning Source LLC
Chambersburg PA
CBHW060805050426
42449CB00008B/1550